RAINBOW
GUITAR

HUGH BOYDE

RAINBOW GUITAR

A colourful approach to teaching and learning guitar from the beginning.
For individual or group tuition. Designed for use at Key Stage 2 or 3.

by Hugh Boyde

Illustrations, layout and design by Kate Molloy of 'Little Designs Cambridge' - www.littledc.co.uk

Published by Ringing Strings
33 Impington Lane, Impington,
Cambridge CB24 9LT
UK

http://www.ringingstringspublications.co.uk

ISBN 978-0-9573503-0-4
Second edition 2012

To the pupil...

There are many, MANY ways to learn and play guitar!
Many kinds of guitar that you can buy.
Many ways of sitting (and standing) with the guitar.
Many ways of plucking and strumming it.
Many ways of learning to understand the notes and chords.
And of course many kinds of music that you can play!

The problem is knowing where to start. This is a simple method for the early stages which works for me and my pupils. I hope you enjoy using it and that you like the music.

The parts of the guitar

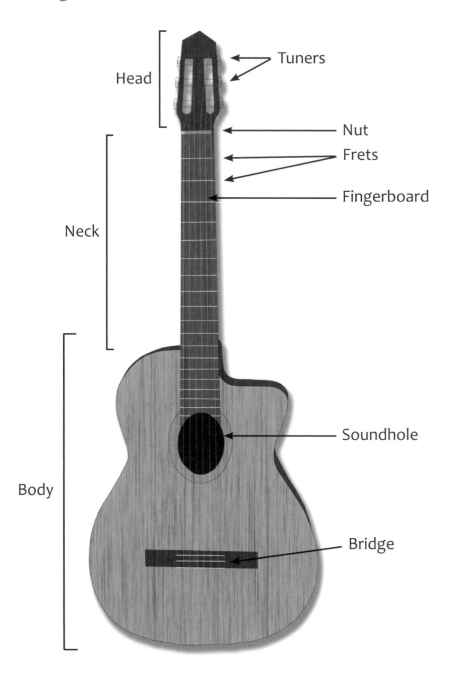

Holding the guitar

The right arm leans on the top of the guitar. Both hands are free - not used to help with holding and balancing the guitar.

The guitar rests on the left leg, tilted upwards at about 45 degrees to the floor.

Wearing a skirt? Try sitting cross-legged instead, with your guitar on your right leg.

The left foot rests on a footstool (or small box or tin).

Numbering and colouring the strings

In this book we are going to learn to play on 2nd, 3rd and 4th strings.
We will give each of these strings a colour:

Green for 2nd
Red for 3rd
Blue for 4th

Put coloured stickers near the bridge of your guitar like this, so you can remind yourself which string is which.

Preparing to pluck

When you are sitting comfortably with the guitar, rest the tips of your index, middle and ring fingers lightly on string 1.

These fingers will steady your hand while you pluck with your thumb.

Let your forearm lean firmly on the top side of the guitar. Let your wrist relax so your thumb and fingers fall loosely towards the strings.

There should be an archway under your wrist as shown.

Now try plucking string 3 (red) with your thumb.

Angle your thumb towards the neck of the guitar, so you can pluck without bumping into your fingers.

Rhythm (quick and slow)

Slow rhythm

Quick rhythm

Mixed rhythm

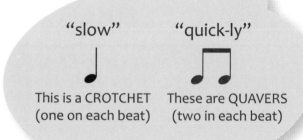

"slow"   "quick-ly"

This is a CROTCHET   These are QUAVERS
(one on each beat)   (two in each beat)

A rhythm tune

Can you play this tune right through and keep your eyes on the page the whole time?

Now try making up a rhythm tune of your own. Take a short rhythm and repeat it on each string in turn as above.

To get some ideas, see if you can find a rhythm in your name, or a friend's name, or in your favourite team, or your favourite food!

The stave

When we write music down, each note is placed on a STAVE which has 5 lines. Each note has its own position on the stave.

Here are our 3 open string notes on the stave:

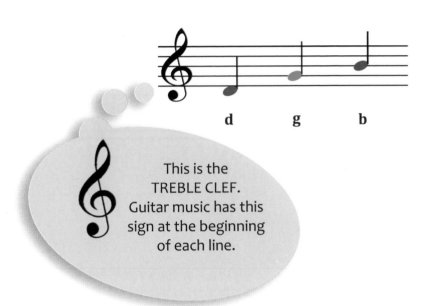

d   g   b

This is the TREBLE CLEF. Guitar music has this sign at the beginning of each line.

The notes are grouped into BARS to make them easier to count. The 2/4 sign means that there are two beats in each bar.

Can you play this tune right through and keep your eyes on the page the whole time?

More tunes with D, G and B

Wake-Up Call

HB

Banjo Tune

HB

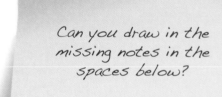

Can you draw in the missing notes in the spaces below?

Note review

g   b   g   g   d   g   b   g   b   g   b   g   d   d   g   g

Easy song accompaniments

Just play the coloured notes. The tune is written in small notes underneath - you can try singing it or perhaps your teacher will sing or play it?

Frere Jacques

London Bridge

"lo-ong"

This is a MINIM and it lasts for 2 beats.

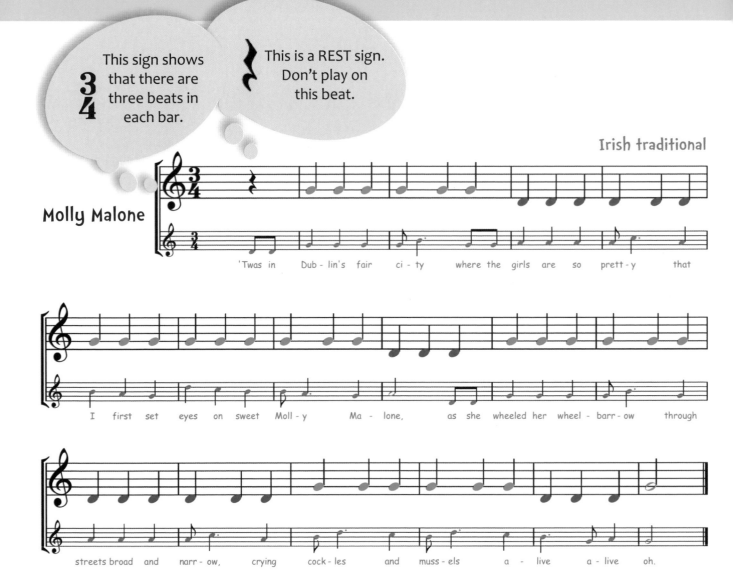

First fretted note (A on the red string)

Press down firmly on the string with the tip of your 2nd finger so that the note rings clearly.

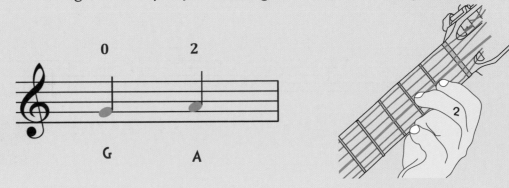

Practice with G and A

You can combine these exercises with the ones on page 16 and page 19 to make mini-duets or trios.

The left hand

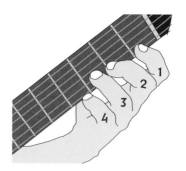

From the front...

You should be able to spread your fingers along one of the strings, into the spaces between the frets, so each finger occupies one space.

...From the back

The pad of the thumb is placed at the centre of the guitar neck, more or less opposite the 2nd finger. The thumb makes a right angle with the neck. The palm of the hand is well away from the neck.

Tunes with G, A and B

The coloured notes are the melody (the most important part!). The small notes underneath are accompaniments to be played by other pupils or your teacher.

EZ: an easy part, sometimes with just open strings
ADV: a part which may contain notes which are learned later in the book

Walking

Hot Cross Buns

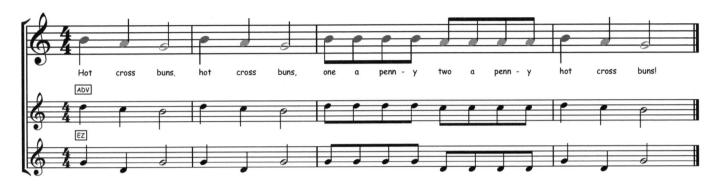

Tunes with D, G, A and B

Hoe Down

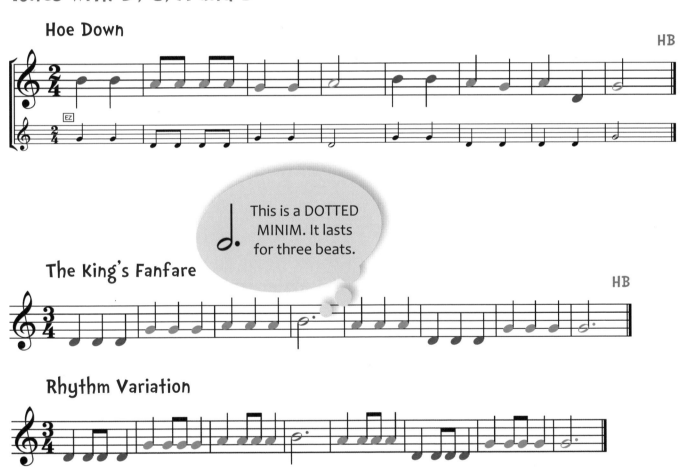

This is a DOTTED MINIM. It lasts for three beats.

The King's Fanfare

Rhythm Variation

Composing: making a variation

Can you make up another rhythm variation for 'The King's Fanfare'? If you can, write it down here and practice it.

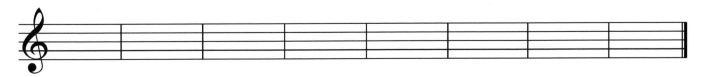

Upbeat Tune

This is the tune played by the famous bells of Big Ben before striking the hour.

Watch out — there is an "extra" beat in each bar, making 5 beats in all!

Big Ben

Note review

d   d   g   a   b   b   a   a   g

Easy song accompaniments

Clementine

American traditional

In a cav-ern in a can-yon ex-ca-va-ting for a mine Lived a

min - er for-ty nin - er and his daught - er Clem-en-tine

Sur le pont d'Avignon

French traditional

Sur le pont d'Av-ign-on l'on y dan-se l'on y dan-se

Sur le pont d'Av-ign-on l'on y dan-se tout en rond.

Another fretted note (E on the blue string)

Press down firmly on the string with the tip of your 2nd finger so that the note rings clearly.

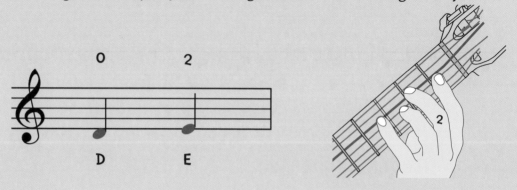

Practice with D and E

You can combine these exercises with the ones on page 11 and page 19 to make mini-duets or trios.

12 Bar Blues

HB

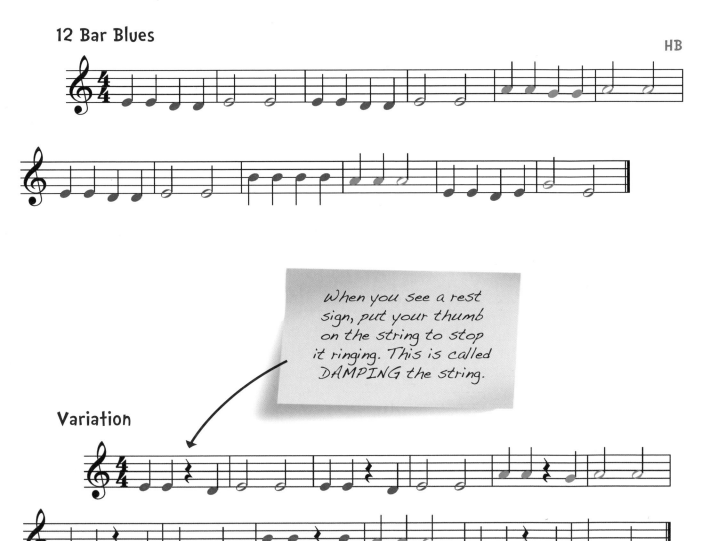

When you see a rest sign, put your thumb on the string to stop it ringing. This is called DAMPING the string.

Variation

An OSTINATO is a short repeated pattern of notes. Ostinatos are often used as accompaniments for tunes or songs.

Fun with ostinatos

Ostinatos are a great way to warm up and practise the notes you have learned. Try some of these patterns. Repeat each one as often as you like. Perhaps your teacher or another pupil can make up a tune to go with it.

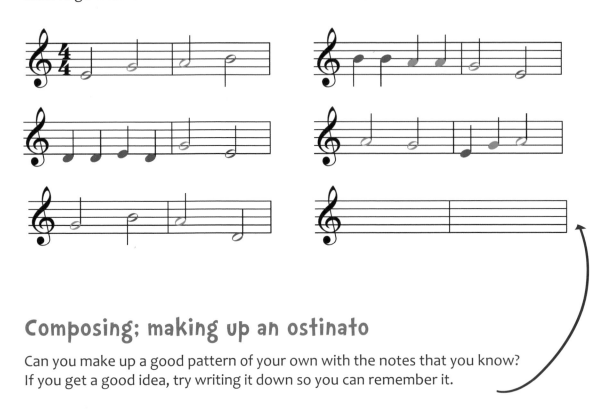

Composing; making up an ostinato

Can you make up a good pattern of your own with the notes that you know?
If you get a good idea, try writing it down so you can remember it.

Composing with a rhythm

Play the rhythm below, on a single note to begin with. Then start to make it into a tune by playing it with more than one note. When you have made up a tune that you like, write down the note names in the spaces under the notes.

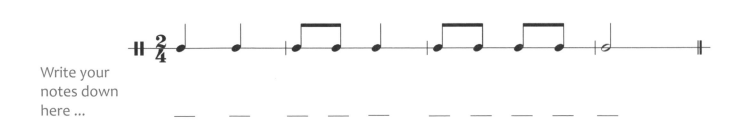

Write your
notes down
here ...

Another fretted note (C on the green string)

Press down firmly on the string with the tip of your 1st finger so that the note rings clearly.

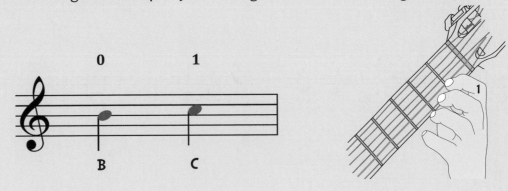

Practice with B and C

You can combine these exercises with the ones on page 11 and page 16 to make mini-duets or trios.

Tunes with G, A, B and C

Scale Practice

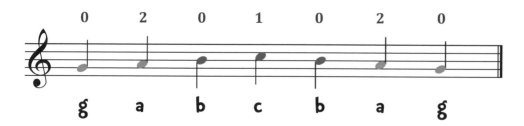

Clog Dance

HB

Pease Pudding Hot

Pease pudd- ing hot, Pease pudd- ing cold Pease pudd- ing in the pot, Nine days old!

Tudor Dance

HB

This is a SEMIBREVE. It lasts for four beats.

Heart's Ease

English traditional

Cowboy Guitars

HB

Composing: questions and answers

Can you make up an ending for these tunes? When you have made up an ending, try and write the notes you have used.
It may help to think of the 1st half of the tune as a question, and the 2nd half as an answer.

Song accompaniments

Aim to make your accompaniment notes ring on and overlap as much as you can manage.

Banks of the Ohio

American traditional

I asked my love   to take a walk   to take a walk

just a litt - le walk   down by the banks   where the wa - ters

flow   down by the banks   of the O - hi - o

Oh Susanna

American traditional

I come from A - la - ba - ma with my ban - jo on my knee   Bound for Louis - i - a - na my own

true love for to see   Oh   Su - sa - nna   oh don't you cry for me   I

come from A - la - ba - ma with my ban - jo on my knee

High D on the green string

Press down firmly on the string with the tip of your 3rd finger so that the note rings clearly.

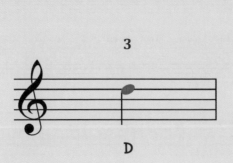

Practice with high D

Siren

Two Sirens

Merrily

Merr - i - ly we roll a - long   roll a - long   roll a - long   Merr - i - ly we roll a - long   Roll - ing through the day

This is a tie sign and joins the two notes together into one longer note.

Amazing Grace

English and American hymn

Tunes with G, A, B, C and D

Scale Practice

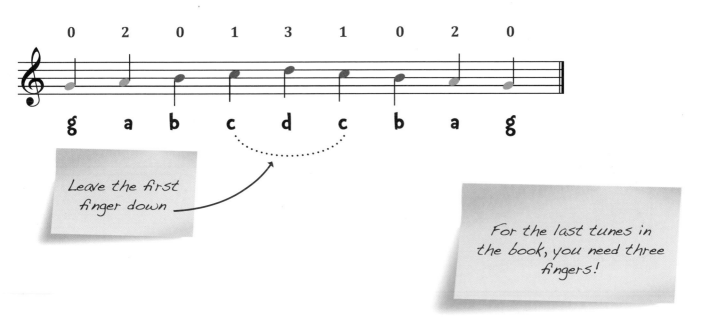

Leave the first finger down

For the last tunes in the book, you need three fingers!

Now The Day Is Over

English hymn

London's Burning (Round)

English traditional

Lon- don's burn - ing   Lon- don's burn - ing   Fetch the   en - gine   Fetch the   en - gine   Fire

fire!   Fire   fire!   Pour on   wat - er   Pour on   wa - ter!

The Cuckoo (Round)

French traditional

La Volta

William Byrd, adapted HB

Shepherd's Hey

English traditional

The notes in this book:

Low D 4th string open	G 3rd string open	B 2nd String open	
E 4th string, 2nd fret	A 3rd string, 2nd fret	C 2nd string, 1st fret	High D 2nd string, 3rd fret

The right hand (for plectrum players)

From the front...

From the back...
The wrist is flat and low over the strings.